GREAT

NEW YORK

RESTAURANTS

GREAT NEW YORK RESTAURANTS

A Photographic Guide

Featuring the photography of

GAYLE GLEASON

Introduction by

JUDD TULLY

Prince Street Editions

L T D

New York

Prince Street Editions, Ltd.
8 Prince Street, New York, N.Y. 10012

Printed in the United States of America.

ISBN: 0-943998-11-5

The typeface used is Goudy Oldstyle.
The book is printed on Vintage Velvet.

Designed by *Randall De Leeuw*

Table of Contents

Publisher's Note

GREAT NEW YORK RESTAURANTS —the title alone brings mouthwatering sensations to the tip of the tongue, and many wonderful memories of splendid breakfasts, lunches and dinners in the not-too-distant past. . .which bring even greater anticipation of those ahead. . . next week, month, year.

GREAT NEW YORK RESTAURANTS is a book intended to stimulate our sensations—first, in the sheer pleasure of so many intriguing, inviting, mysterious, colorful, even fantastic interior spaces. Included are historic and contemporary, classic French, Italian, ethnic and American, neighborhood pubs and celebrity gathering places, magnificent vistas and intimate dining rooms. Each photograph is an open invitation to come inside, relax, and enjoy the many varied dining experiences only this great city can offer.

Congratulations to photographer Gayle Gleason. Her remarkable photographs reveal the intimate, insider's view. With patience and determination, she has captured the warmth, character, and, yes, even the aroma of these fine establishments. No small achievement.

And salutations to the hardworking restaurateurs whose establishments are featured. New York would not be a gastronomic center of international fame without their individual dedication to excellence.

Randall De Leeuw

New York
April, 1986

Featured Restaurants

Andrée's Mediterranean Cuisine
Angelo's
Avgerino's
Barbetta
Berry's
Binghamton's
Black Sheep
Cafe Luxembourg
Caffe Roma
Caramba
The Carlyle Restaurant
Cinco de Mayo
Claire
La Colombe d'Or
Le Cygne
Dish of Salt
Fay & Allen's Catch of the Sea
Fonda La Paloma
Gage & Tollner
Garvin's
Gian Marino
Hamburger Harry's
Harvey's Chelsea Restaurant
Il Cortile
Joanna
Joanna (The Nightclub)
The Jockey Club
Keens
The Landmark Tavern
Laurent
Lavin's
Lion's Rock
La Louisiana
Maxwell's Plum
Manhattan Cafe
Moran's
The Odeon
Oh Ho So
One Fifth
One If By Land, Two If By Sea
The Oyster Bar & Restaurant
Peacock Alley
Les Pleiades
The Quilted Giraffe
Raoul's
Le Reginette
The River Club
Roebling's
Roxanne's
Russell's
65 Irving Place
Suerken's
Tennessee Mountain
The Terrace Restaurant
Texarkana
Le Train Bleu
Tre Scalini
Vanessa
Victor's Café 52
Windows on the World

A restored view of the candlelit Long Room at Fraunces Tavern, site of General George Washington's farewell to his officers in 1783. Courtesy of Fraunces Tavern Museum, New York.

Fast food dining took a great leap forward with the Automat. Circa 1940.

Looking Backwards at Some Manhattan Eateries

A perfect lunchtime appetizer in Manhattan's Financial District is a trip to the Fraunces Tavern Museum at the corners of Broad and Pearl streets. Upstairs, just past the hungry line of diners, is the Long Room of Fraunces Tavern, site of General George Washington's noon-time farewell to 44 of his Revolutionary War officers on December 4, 1783. The standing bar and plain tables covered with checker boards and long stemmed, white clay pipes bring you back to that extraordinary time. Perhaps General Washington drank rum-laced fruit punch from a pewter mug, supplied by proprietor Samuel Fraunces, who became Washington's official steward during the first year of his presidency. But that is jumping the gun. The officers drank and bid a teary farewell to their chief and saw him off to board a boat at nearby Whitehall.

Set in the doorway of the Long Room, an illuminated information panel tells you that drinking was the primary recreation of the 18th century tavern. Merchants could smoke their pipes, read English newspapers and peer through conveniently placed "spyglasses" to monitor arrivals and departures of ships in the harbor. Only the tinkling sounds of silverware tapping china from the restaurant below break the reverie.

New York City has 32 pages of restaurant listings in the Yellow Pages, from the A B C Snack Bar to Zum Zum's. No doubt some have already perished or changed locations. The *New York Times* will grill or praise a restaurant or two every Friday while a host of slick magazines will investigate a new venture's decor, decibel level, grammar of the help and the crispness of the napkin's crease before volunteering a word on the food. There are television critics and hefty guidebooks to steer you to a particular place. This essay will touch upon a number of establishments that have long since faded from view. Their separate and sometimes eccentric histories are a part of New York that novelists and painters strive to capture.

The remarkable writer Stephen Crane (best known for his *Red Badge of Courage*) prowled the streets of Manhattan in the late 1800's and wrote about some wonderful characters who inhabited the Bowery and Tenderloin. Crane described the manic action "In a Park Row Restaurant" for the daily readers of the *New York Press* this way on October 28, 1894: "There was in the air an endless clatter of dishes, loud and bewilderingly rapid, like the gallop of a thousand horses. From afar back, at the places of communication to the kitchen, there came the sound of a continual roaring altercation, hoarse and vehement, like the cries of the officers of a regiment under attack. A mist of steam fluttered where the waiters crowded and jostled about the huge copper coffee urns."

Crane was writing about a "fast-food" establishment called "The Boeuf-a-la-mode" which he and his friends re-named, "The Buffalo Mud." The story's hero, an ex-sheriff from the wilds of Nevada, suggests that the waiters—in order to speed service—be outfitted with repeating rifles to shoot "the corn muffins, butter cakes, Irish stews or any delicacy of the season." We immediately learn that New Yorkers have always been an impatient lot, bent on dispatching their victuals in record time.

It is easy to jump from Crane's waiters outfitted with repeating rifles to a 1940's picture of a Horn & Hardart Automat Cafeteria where both men and women jockey for position at the glass cases chock full of 25 cent sandwiches and baked bean casseroles. From a fortress of cakes and pies to a polished wolf's head spigot dispensing rivers of hot coffee, the Automat's miniature locked doors opened at the drop of a few nickels. At one time, there were 26 Automats in Manhattan, all open between 7 A.M. and 1 A.M., every day. The vintage image, especially the lady in the striped suit, balancing a slippery ear of corn on a cafeteria plate, emphatically tells you the Automat catered to every class and fashion. The Smithsonian's National Museum of American Art in Washington, D.C. thought enough of this mostly bygone phenomena to install an entire Automat wall as one of their permanent exhibits. You can still visit a Horn & Hardart at the corner of 42nd and 3rd Avenue.

Digging into the hungry past of New York reveals both plebian and patrician tastes. An engraved illustration from an 1882 issue of *Frank Leslie's Illustrated Newspaper* portrays a formally fitted waiter in muttonchop whiskers, serving a heavily gowned and black-tailed group of diners under an elaborate gaslit chandelier. The table is crowded with long stemmed crystal and the dining chairs are plump with upholstery. Contrasted to this luxurious image, the second panel of the illustration is bareboned and the chairs cushionless. A grim-faced waiter elbows his way through a sea of impatient diners armed with raised table knives. From the posh restaurant to the all night "coffee and cake saloon," New Yorkers consumed every imaginable dish, from truffled paté of imported hare to pig's head with cabbage and turnips.

In what might have been one of the earliest restaurant reviews, a reporter for *Harper's Weekly* summed up his experience at the Penny Restaurant on Grand Street: "The one cent portions are small, yet a fair appetite could be appeased for five cents, and a ravenous one for ten." The 1877 review mentioned lamb pot-pie for five cents, boiled rice for one cent and a quarter of apple pie for three cents. The enthusiastic critic also noted that "cheap and nasty does not apply to this establishment."

The March 4, 1882 issue of Frank Leslie's Illustrated Newspaper depicts the sharp contrast between eating classes. Courtesy of The New-York Historical Society, New York.

The sandwich board of The Penny Restaurant attracts a following. From the pen of illustrator William A. Rogers. Harper's Weekly, December 8, 1877. Courtesy of the New York Public Library.

Delmonico's ritzy headquarters on 5th Avenue and 26th Street before their final move uptown to 44th Street. Courtesy of The New-York Historical Society, New York.

A well-hoofed stag party at the luxurious Louis Sherry's at Fifth Avenue and 44th Street in the early 1900's.

The fabulously appointed Louis Sherry Restaurant on 5th Avenue and 44th Street was designed by the famous American architect Stanford White in 1898 (McKim, Mead & White had already built Madison Square Garden, a full block pleasure palace, complete with restaurant and roof-garden cabaret). Sherry proved to be serious competition for Delmonico's, New York's first gourmet restaurant created for the wealthy. In the early 1900's, Sherry's served a bachelor banquet hosted by Cornelius K. Billingsworth in one of the establishment's private ball rooms. The guests, stiff in formal attire, drank and ate while mounted on horseback. Waiters were costumed as grooms and busboys scurried around the campfire formation, cleaning up after the restless horses. With a tromp l'oeil backdrop of English gardens and enough champagne to flood a stable, the boisterous assembly would have impressed promoter P.T. Barnum.

In her article on "Famous American Restaurants and Some of the Delicacies for which they are Noted," that appeared in the January, 1909 issue of *Good House Keeping*, Amy Lyman Philips wrote that "Delmonico's is the favorite restaurant of the ultra-conservative in New York." One tends to believe her and the fading photographs that accompany the article show a lot of thick carpeting, secluded, palm shaded corners and acres of velvet curtains. Philips divided New York into three restaurant classes: the "ultrafashionable" establishments on 5th Avenue, "The gay, all-nite restaurants patronized by the after-theatre crowd," and the "foreign spots" representing German, Hungarian, Spanish, Mexican, French, Italian, Greek, Russian and Chinese cuisines. Philips urged her readers to try Cafe Lafayette on University Place and 9th Street, "patronized a great deal by foreigners especially during the dinner or luncheon hour, when one sees a dozen or more taxi cabs drawn up to deposit the beautifully gowned women and men in correct evening clothes who come down sometimes from their own luxurious up-town hotels to have a real French dinner." Even then, New Yorkers were willing to go out of their way for a good meal.

Philips praised the chestnut soup and leather cushioned seats along the wall at Mouqin's but noted the place was more interesting at night. You can get a taste of that atmosphere today with a visit to the Art Institute of Chicago where William J. Glackens' festive "Chez Mouqin" stars in a gallery devoted to early 20th century American art. Glackens' 1905 picture celebrates the well-heeled night life of the theatre crowd. The prosperous looking couple toast their good fortune and the mirror behind them reflects the sea of colorful gowns and bustling waiters.

If one's budget could not manage "Chicken ala Marengo" at Mouqin's, a 60 cent dinner was available downtown at the Cafe Boulevard on Second Avenue and 10th Street. Miss Philips, never out of step, praised the restaurant's Hungarian Gypsy band and "the many queer dishes that rivals the food of Italy." The cast-iron and glass hood of Cafe Boulevard, located next door to the famed Manhattan School of Music, welcomed 1,000 diners daily. Aided with a magnifying glass, the charming old photograph reveals a parked, horse-drawn van loaded with freshly laundered barbers' towels. A billboard across the street asked, "How is Your Tongue?" and recommended Partola lozenges, "The Doctor in Candy Form."

With the double allure of Hungarian Goulash and authentic gypsy music, Cafe Boulevard was, as Miss Philips observed, "a bright spot on the grim east side." The cafe was a perfect respite after a matinee or evening performance at the popular Yiddish theatre on the corner of Second Avenue and 12th Street.

Before the austere hand of the Volstead Act snuffed out wine cellars and gin fizzes in 1919, a number of wild emporiums, like Murray's Roman Gardens on 42nd Street and Broadway appeared in an unbelievable display of ostentation. The Theatre District and the Great White Way were in full bloom and restaurateurs were beginning to learn, like their Hollywood counterparts to follow, that the spectacle, Cecil B. DeMille style, was profitable. Murray's resembled such a Hollywood set with no expenses spared. It was as if Liberace were asked to recreate Pompei without scholarly consultation. Mosaics and mirrors dominated the subterranean behemoth and enchantingly costumed harem girls and turbaned minstrels roamed the restaurant. Commenting on the devastating effect of the Federal Volstead Act, Michael and Ariane Batterberry, in their delightful book "On the Town in New York," wrote about the last days of Murray's: "Bartenders stood with trembling lips behind bars, while their patrons openly wept into their drinks." Murray's was converted into a flea circus.

The speakeasy took off to counter the no-fun abstinence of Prohibition and private clubs sprouted throughout the city. Some of the pricier spots boasted camouflaged wine cellars. More modest establishments, like the Pepper Pot in Greenwich Village, gave the appearance of a Bohemian joint, complete with melting candles stuck in old beer bottles. To enjoy the reputed artistic flavor, diners endured subdued light, hard-backed chairs and a dangling assortment of trinkets hanging from the ceiling heating pipe. "Slumming" in exotic neighborhoods became a respected pastime.

Reginald Marsh, the great American artist who sketched and painted New York from the Bowery to Coney Island, etched a powerful little print, "Speakeasy-Julius' Annex" in 1929. Marsh shows us a no-frills room with a quartet of round tables occupied by couples in various stages of inebriation. A slouch-shouldered waiter shuffles through the room with a tray of drinks and the atmosphere fairly screams with despair. Through the curtained entry-way in the back of the room, a medly of male heads continue the impression of slurred banter. Always a social commentator, Marsh brusquely stated the impending Great Depression in the faces of the drinkers.

American painter William J. Glackens captures the nighttime flavor of Chez Mouquin in 1905. Courtesy of the Art Institute of Chicago.

The Hollywood spectacle invades Murray's Roman Gardens on 42nd Street. Prohibition put an end to the spirit of Bacchus.

Cafe Boulevard on Second Avenue and 10th Street attracted 1,000 diners daily for the exotic Hungarian fare and live Gypsy music.

An entirely different picture of the times can be found in Edward Hopper's painting, "Chop Suey," from the same year. Instead of harsh, artificial light, Hopper's interior is awash with sunlight. The two women diners in their snug fitting "flapper" hats sit at a marble topped table, ready to pour some Chinese tea. Hopper hunted meditative interiors and was a master at depicting the style of the time, whether it be a bobbed blonde or a regimental display of fresh grapefruits. The old fashioned cash register and glass case brimming with open cigar boxes form a convincing chronicle of the changing times.

It would be a delight to return to some of those spots, whether real or imagined, from the pen of Stephen Crane to the brush of Edward Hopper. Or dust off an old menu from the Hotel St. Andre located at 11th Street near Broadway that boasted of "the very best French and American cooks," a kind of precursor to the just passed rage of "nouvelle cuisine." The new proprietors at the St. Andre "Americanized" their menu "to serve better meals for the price than any restaurant in the city." The red corners of the old hotel menu break off at the touch. The reader remains charmed at a note placed at the bottom of the menu card, earmarked to "Ladies Shopping: This restaurant offers special inducements as a quiet, genteel resort. A cordial invitation is extended to all to try us and test the truth of our assertions."

The great restaurateurs then and now attempted to bewitch their customer whether by price, taste or atmosphere. Some of the great ones, like Louis Sherry, had to close their doors despite phenomenal success. Sherry blamed his demise on "prohibition and war-born Bolshevism." When his long-time arch rival, Delmonico's, finally expired in 1923, after a hundred years of continuous operation, it was the bulldozer and not Bolshevism that caused its wrought iron covered doors to shut.

As a last image in this brief chronicle of Manhattan eateries, Jack's Famous Oyster grill stands proudly under the dark iron work of the old 6th Avenue elevated. Despite the "no parking here" sign, a stately 1930-era Ford Model T hugs the curb, poised for a fast get-a-way. We can only imagine the interior and succulent aromas of roasting oysters and strong ale, two standbys that trace a gustatory trail back to the days of Samuel Fraunces. The handsome glass and cast iron front of the restaurant is masculine and inviting. Stencilled signs on the second story windows inform us that a costumer and surgeon-dentist are instantly available. Jack's—like the rumbling elevated line and pristine Ford—has taken its position in history. The curtained windows of the restaurant still beckon. Let's step inside.

Judd Tully
New York
April 1986

Jack's Famous Oyster House disappeared along with the Sixth Avenue Elevated despite their cast-iron constitutions.

Sources:

Batterberry, Michael and Ariane, "On the Town in New York, a history of eating, drinking and entertainments from 1776 to the present," Charles Scribner's Sons, New York, 1973.

Edmiston, Susan and Cirino, Linda D., "Literary New York—a History and Guide," Houghton Mifflin Company, Boston, 1976.

Hart, Harold H., "Hart's Guide to New York City," Hart Publishing Company, New York, 1964.

Levin, Gail, "Edward Hopper," Crown Publishers, Inc., New York, 1984.

Sasowsky, Norman, "The Prints of Reginald Marsh," Clarkson N. Potter, Inc., New York, 1970.

Silver, Nathan, "Lost New York," American Legacy Press by arrangement with Houghton Mifflin Company, 1967. New York.

Stallman, R.W. and Hagemann, E.R., "The New York City Sketches of Stephen Crane," New York University Press, New York, 1966.

The author would like to specially thank Michael Batterberry for his kind and informative assistance.

FEATURED RESTAURANTS

ANDRÉE'S MEDITERRANEAN CUISINE
354 East 74th Street
New York, N.Y. 10021
(212) 249-6619

Come to this gem of a townhouse restaurant on Manhattan's Upper East Side. Let award-winning Master Chef Andrée take a few minutes away from the stove to introduce you to her spirited, sunny cuisine inspired by Provence, the Riviera, Greece and Morocco, to which she has added her own touches.

Lunch, Tuesday, Wednesday, Thursday, 12:00 - 2:00.
Dinner Tuesday - Saturday, 6:00 - 10:00.
Reservations required. Private parties.
American Express.
Wine and beer only.

MENU SELECTIONS

Appetizers

Kobeba (meat-filled wheat shells)
Taramosalata (Greek caviar dip)
Tabbouleh (bulgur, scallions, mint & parsley salad)

First Courses

Merguez au Fromage
(homemade lamb sausage with fried cheese)
Shrimp Alexandria
(flambéed with ouzo, tomatoes & feta)

Main Courses

Cassoulet
Canard au Poivre Vert
Couscous Amal
Couscous au Poisson
Rack of Lamb Méditerranée

Desserts

Pears in Chablis
Mocha Crème Royale

ANGELO'S
of Mulberry Street
146 Mulberry Street
New York, N.Y. 10013
(212) 966-1277

Finest Neapolitan cuisine. Your Hosts: Gino & Giovanni.
Closed Monday.
Reservations accepted for four or more.
All major credit cards.

MENU SELECTIONS

Appetizers

Antipasto Di Mare
Spedini di Mozzarella Alla Romana
Eggplant Sciué Sciué

Entrees

Striped Bass Alla Riviera
Veal Scaloppine Alla Capresa
Scaloppini Filet Mignon Alla Angelo
Boneless Chicken Alla Scarpariello
Shrimps Alla Angelo

Desserts

Zabaglione with Imported marsala
Torta di Cioccolata

AVERGINOS
at Citicorp Center Market
between Lexington & 3rd Avenues and
53rd & 54th Streets, New York, N.Y. 10022
(212) 688-8828

Averginos Greek restaurant was built in 1977 by architect Anestis Demou. Located on the plaza level of Citicorp Center Market, Avgerinos offers one of New York's unique dining experiences. Authentic and inexpensive dishes are prepared before your eyes. Catering.

Open 7 days, 11:30 am - 11 pm.
Reservations are not necessary.
All major credit cards.

MENU SELECTIONS

Appetizers

Stuffed grape leaves
Mushrooms a la Grecque
Mixed hot mezedakia

Entrees

Chicken, lamb or seafood souvlaki
Moussaka
Exochiko
Pastitsio
Roast leg of lamb

Desserts

Baklava
Galaktoboureko

BARBETTA
321 West 46th Street
New York, N.Y. 10036
(212) 246-9171

Opened in 1906, Barbetta is New York's oldest restaurant still owned by the family that founded it. Decorated with authentic 18th century Italian furnishings, Barbetta serves the cuisine of Italy's northernmost province, Piemonte. In summer, its exhuberantly romantic garden, flowering and verdant, is one of the most sought after dining sites in the city. Private rooms available.

Open for lunch, 12 noon - 2 pm; dinner 5:30 pm til midnight. Closed Sunday.
Reservations are suggested.
All major credit cards.

MENU SELECTIONS

Appetizers

Mushroom Salad alla Schobert
Bagna Cauda

Pasta

Risotto Piemontese
Fonduta with fresh white truffles

Main Courses

Baby Salmon saute with Butter and Parsley
Fresh Crabmeat saute in Sherry with Wild Rice
Bolliti Misti Piemontesi
Vitel Tonné
Carne Cruda alla Piemontese
Bue al Barolo

Desserts

Monte Bianco
Raspberry Tart

BERRY'S
180 Spring Street
New York, N.Y. 10012
(212) 226-4394

Berry sees her restaurant as a convivial extension of her living room, where a changing menu reflects seasonal availability and interests of the chef, and well-mixed drinks and carefully chosen wines are presented by a courteous and professional staff.

Open for lunch, Tuesday - Friday, Brunch & Sunday,
Dinner Tuesday - Sunday.
Reservations are suggested.
American Express, Mastercard, Visa.

MENU SELECTIONS

Appetizers

Onion Tart
Caesar Salad

Entrees

Straw & Hay Scampi
Lamb Chops Bretonne
Calves Liver with Shallots
Crabby Chicken
Steak Tartare
Filet Mignon

Desserts

Bananas Foster
Profiteroles

BINGHAMTON'S
Moored on the Hudson River
Overlooking the New York Skyline
3 miles south of the George Washington Bridge
(201) 941-2300

Enjoy landmark dining in a landmark setting. The Binghamton is an elegantly restored Victorian ferryboat adorned with the brass and stained-glass fittings of a bygone era. She is the only double-ender steam engine ferryboat still floating in the Hudosn River. Party accommodations available.

Open 7 days a week, 12 noon - 2 am.
Reservations are not necessary.
All major credit cards.

Listed in the National Register of Historic Places

MENU SELECTIONS

Appetizers

Neptune Antipasto
Baked Stuffed Clams
Tortellini

Entrees

Carpetbag Steak
Chicken Amaretto
Stuffed Shrimp
Lobster
Chicken & Crab Mandarin

Desserts

Ice Cream Sundaes
Gooseberry Tart

THE BLACK SHEEP
344 West 11th Street
New York, N.Y. 10014
(212) 242-1010

This is the romantic "Village" neighborhood restaurant one searches for and so rarely finds. You'll dine in a cozy, intimate atmosphere of brick walls, candles, drying herbs and an old stove that holds the evening's rich, homemade desserts. Still sporting the tin ceiling from its former life as a pool hall, The Black Sheep's seasonal menu features hearty dishes of Burgundy and Provence, and an emphasis on nutritionally balanced lighter dishes. One of the city's finest wine lists.

Dinner daily from 6 pm, Sunday brunch noon - 4 pm.
Reservations are recommended.
All major credit cards.

MENU SELECTIONS

Price fixed six course dinner

Crudites of fresh & marinated vegetables

Choice of two soups

French Country style paté

Loin Rack of Lamb
Duckling cooked two ways
Norwegian Salmon filet
Fresh pasta of the day

Tossed salad with vinaigrette dressing

Choice from the Dessert table

CAFE LUXEMBOURG
200 West 70th Street
New York, N.Y. 10023
(212) 873-7411

Open Monday - Thursday 5:30 - 12:30 pm; Friday & Saturday 6:00 pm - 1:30 am; Sunday 6 - 12:30 am; Saturday Brunch 12 - 3, Sunday Brunch 11 - 3.
Reservations: Recommended.
American Express, Mastercard, Visa.

MENU SELECTIONS

Appetizers

Smoked salmon and crackling salad
Carpaccio with a dijonaise sauce

Entrees

Cajun style brook trout
Paillard of chicken
Sauteed calfs liver
Crisp roasted duckling with a ginger baked pear
Grilled filet mignon

Desserts

Maple pecan tart
Creme brulee

CAFFÉ ROMA
385 Broome Street
New York, N.Y. 10013
(212) 226-8413

Caffé Roma exemplifies Old World charm. Many of the original antiques, especially the mahogany and brass grandfather clock, are part of the charming decor. A wide assortment of Italian pastries is prepared according to tradition. The atmosphere is casual, setting the mood of a European cafe. House specialties have received gourmet acclaim.

Sunday - Thursday, 8 am - midnight.
Friday & Saturday til 1:00 am.

MENU SELECTIONS

Espresso & cappucino
Spumoni, tartufo, gelati

Assorted pastries
Cannoli Siciliana
Pasticciotto a Riccotta
Napoleon
Baba a Rhum
Italian cheese cake

CARAMBA I
918 Eighth Avenue
New York, N.Y. 10019
(212) 245-7910

CARAMBA II
Broadway & 3rd Street
New York, N.Y. 10012
(212) 420-9817

CARAMBA III
Broadway & 96th Street
New York, N.Y. 10025
(212) 749-5055

Serving authentic peasant foods from Mexico and the American Southwest plus potent, slush Margaritas, Caramba's menu goes from "The Ridiculous" 28-ounce Margarita to its sublime array of great dishes. Without doubt, Caramba offers the best Mexican food East of the West.

Open 7 days, 12 noon - midnight, Saturday & Sunday brunch, 12 noon - 4 pm.
Reservations suggested.
American Express, Diners Club, Mastercard, Visa.

MENU SELECTIONS

Appetizers

Nachos
Flautas
Taquitos

Entrees

Taco, Enchilada, Relleno, Burrito combinations
Chimichanga
Bocados Amores
Enchiladas Verdes

Desserts

Homemade flan
Kahlua mousse
Sopaipillas

THE CARLYLE RESTAURANT
The Carlyle Hotel
35 East 76th Street
New York, N.Y. 10021
(212) 744-1600

New classic French cuisine—the freshest and most choice ingredients are used, and the setting retains the high style of New York's most gracious days.

Monday - Saturday Breakfast, 7 - 11 am; Luncheon, 12 - 2:30 pm; Dinner 6 - 11 pm.
Sunday Breakfast, 8 - 10:30 am; Brunch, 12 - 3 pm; Dinner 6 - 11 pm.
Reservations are recommended.
All major credit cards.

MENU SELECTIONS

Appetizers

Homemade Terrine of Fresh Foie Gras with Port
Artichoke Mousse with Medaillons of Lobster
Gazpacho Andalouse

Entrees

Sauteed Dover Sole with Pistachio Nuts
Lobster and Truffles with Fettuccine and Fresh Basil
Feuillete of Sweetbreads
Sauteed Veal Chop served with
a Compote of Eggplant
Escallop of Norwegian Salmon with
a Vermouth and Cucumber Sauce

Desserts

Hot Raspberry Souffle
Assorted Pastries from our Dessert Trolley

CINCO DE MAYO
349 West Broadway
New York, N.Y. 10013
(212) 226-5255

Enjoy New York's only three sombrero Mexican restaurant, located in Soho, where artists, playwrights, and actors meet to enjoy authentic Mexican cuisine and "lethal" margaritas. Skylit dining rooms.

Lunch and dinner daily, noon to midnight.
Special brunch on Saturday and Sunday, 11 am - 4 pm.
Facilities for private parties.
Reservations are suggested.
All major credit cards.

MENU SELECTIONS

Appetizers

Camarones
Taquitos de Moronga
Guacamole

Entrees

Chiles Rellenos
Pollo en Salsa de Cacahuate
Pescado en Salsa de Chile Poblano
Chuletas de Puerco Adobadas

Desserts

Flan Yucateco
Carlota de Chocolate

CLAIRE
156 Seventh Avenue
New York, N.Y. 10011
(212) 255-1955

A lively, informal restaurant with a distinctly tropical tone. The specialty is seafood, including selections from tropical waters. The invariably fresh menu changes daily. The wine list is moderately priced.

Open seven days for lunch and dinner.
Reservations are recommended.
American Express, Visa, Mastercard.

MENU SELECTIONS

Appetizers

Seviche of Fresh Tuna
Roasted Andouille Sausages
Bahamian Conch Chowder

Entrees

Broiled fillet of Wahoo
Broiled fillet of Key West Grouper "Provencale"
Baked fresh Red Snapper with shrimp, scallops & crabmeat in parchment "Cajun Style"
Pan-fried Virginia River Catfish
Blackened Redfish, a New Orleans specialty

Desserts

Fresh Key Lime Pie
Mississippi Mud Cake with Whiskey Sauce
Warm Pineapple Cobbler with Vanilla Ice Cream

LA COLOMBE D'OR
134-6 East 26th Street
(between Lexington and Third Avenue)
New York, N.Y. 10010
(212) 689-0666

The award winning Colombe d'Or is a touch of Provence in mid-Manhattan. Regional foods and wines of southern France are the specialty including bouillabaisse and cassoulet. The Napoleon Room is available for private parties.

Open for lunch Monday - Friday, noon - 2:30 pm; open for dinner Monday - Saturday, 6 pm to 11 pm.
Reservations recommended.
All major credit cards.

MENU SELECTIONS

Appetizers

Escargots Maison
Crepes d'Aubergines

Entrees

Pasta au Saumon Fumé
Medaillons de Lotte au Safran
Bouillabaisse Maison
Roti d'Agneau aux Herbes
Tournedos aux Chanterelles et Madeire

Desserts

Fresh Selection Daily

LE CYGNE
55 East 54th Street
New York, N.Y. 10022
(212) 759-5941

Serving the finest classical French cuisine. The Trianon Room.

Serving lunch Monday - Friday, noon - 2:30 pm; dinner Monday - Thursday, 6 - 9:30 pm, Friday & Saturday till 11 pm. Closed Sunday and all major holidays.
Reservations are required.
All major credit cards.

MENU SELECTIONS

Appetizers

Terrine de Canard
Fricassee de Crevettes Roses Grassoises

Entrees

Gateau De Homard Nantua
Thon Roti au Capres, Citron et Tomates
Selle D'Agneau Farcie Jus A L'Estragon
Cassoulet au Lentilles Verte du Puy
Medaillon de Lotte au Trois Sauce

Dessert

Sorbets aux Fruits
Mousses
Souffles Tous Parfums

DISH OF SALT
133 West 47th Street (between 6th & 7th)
New York, N.Y. 10036
(212) 921-4242

Multi-level contemporary restaurant provides ideal setting in Manhattan's theatre district for outstanding Cantonese cuisine and great keyboard artistry.

Open Monday - Friday, 11:30 am - midnight. Saturday & Sunday, 4 pm - midnight.
Reservations are recommended.
American Express, Diners Club.

MENU SELECTIONS

Appetizers

Fried Coconut Prawns
Baked Oysters stuffed with Coriander & Bacon

Entrees

Braised Filet of Gray Sole with Ginger & Scallion
Spicy Angry Chicken
Dish of Salt Marinated Steak
Steamed Lobster with Ginger & Scallion
Four Season Mushrooms with Snow Peas

Desserts

Varied selections

FAY & ALLEN'S CATCH OF THE SEA
1240 Third Avenue (at 72nd Street)
New York, N.Y. 10021
(212) 472-9666

"One of the most beautiful seafood restaurants in New York City."
—*Cue Magazine*

"If lobster's on your mind, you'll find them fresh, tender and delicious."
—*Forbes Magazine*

Open Monday - Thursday, 12 noon - 10:00 pm; Friday & Saturday til 11 pm; Sunday til 9 pm.
Reservations are advisable.
All major credit cards.

MENU SELECTIONS

Appetizers

Herring Filets, Cream Sauce
Smoked Fresh Lake Sturgeon

Entrees

Broiled Prime Sirloin Steak
Broiled Filet of Grey Sole
Block Island Sea Bass, Almondine
Whole Idaho Rainbow Trout
Grilled Swordfish Steak

Desserts

Chocolate Fudge Blackout Cake
Hot Homemade Pecan Pie

FONDA LA PALOMA
26 East 49th Street
New York N.Y. 10017
(212) 421-5495

The charm and cuisine of Old Mexico can be found daily at Fonda La Paloma. Inside the lovely townhouse setting, diners are serenaded by strolling guitarists (Mon. - Sat.) while enjoying authentic Mexican specialties.

Open 7 days a week.
Lunch Monday - Friday, Dinner Monday - Sunday
Reservations suggested.
All major credit cards accepted.

MENU SELECTIONS

Appetizers

Quesadilla
Nachos con Frijoles Refritos
Sopa de Frijoles Negros

Entrees

Mexican combination platters
Enchiladas Suizas
Carne Asada
Chiles Rellenos
Camarones a la Fonda

Desserts

Flan
Guayaba con Queso de Crema
Mangos

GAGE & TOLLNER
Established 1879
372 Fulton Mall near Boro Hall
Brooklyn, N.Y. 11201
(718) 875-5181

Famous for seafood and chops. A 107 year old landmark near the end of the Brooklyn Bridge. Free parking, all subways close by.

Open Monday - Friday 12 noon - 9:30 pm, Saturday 4 - 10:30 pm.
Closed Sunday.
Reservations suggested.
All major credit cards.

First New York City commercial interior designated a landmark.

MENU SELECTIONS

Appetizers

Soft Clam Bellies
Oysters Rockefeller
Lobster Bisque

Entrees

Oysters, Celery Cream Broil
Bay Scallops, Coquilles St. Jacques
Shrimp Creole (with Rice)
Alaskan King Crab Legs
Boned Bluefish
Lobster Thermidor
Sirloin Steak for 2

Desserts

Varied selections

GARVIN'S RESTAURANT
19 Waverly Place
New York, N.Y. 10003
(212) 473-5261

Garvin's restaurant embraces you lovingly with a gracious ambiance—courteous service, elegant decor and fabulous food. The wine list is extensive and very reasonably priced. The pastry chef is without rival in Greenwich Village.

Pre-theatre dinner, 5 - 7 pm; open Tuesday - Sunday for lunch and dinner, Sunday brunch. Jazz nightly.
Reservations suggested.
All major credit cards.

MENU SELECTIONS

Appetizers

Julienne of Smoked Chicken
Mussels Steamed with Champagne
Shrimp, Scallop & Snowpea Salad

Entrees

Sauteed Yellowtail Flounder
Grilled Filet Mignon
Shellfish Louisianne
Roast Cornish Game Hen
Roast Duckling Valencia

Desserts

Creme Caramel
Strawberry Shortcake
Raspberry Beret

GIAN MARINO
221 East 58th Street
New York, N.Y. 10022
(212) 752-1696; 753-8480

Famous 3-Star restaurant, featuring authentic specialties from the 20 provinces of Italy. A favorite of Sophia Loren and other celebrities.

Open Tuesday - Friday, 12 noon - midnight; Saturday 4 pm - midnight, Sunday 1 pm - midnight.
Reservations suggested.
All major credit cards.

MENU SELECTIONS

Appetizers

Eggplant Rollantine
Mussels or Clams Posillipo
Scampi Alla Moda Dei Frati

Pasta

Fusilli Alla Papalina
Fettucine Puttanesca

Entrees

Rosette Di Pollo Alla Massimo
Veal Scaloppine Alla Boscaiola
Filet Mignon Rollatine
Striped Bass Alpescatore
Lobster Fra Diavolo
Sweetbreads Alla Patty

Desserts

Ganache
Cassino
Gelato Tartufo

HAMBURGER HARRY'S (HA HA's)

157 Chambers Street
New York, N.Y. 10007
(212) 267-4446

145 West 45th Street
New York, N.Y. 10036
(212) 840-0566

A casual burger cafe serving 17 varieties of hamburgers, grilled over charcoal and mesquite. Southwestern-style chili, daily "blue plate" specials, soups, salads, fajitas, sandwiches and double rich chocolate malteds are house specialties. Catering.

Open Monday - Saturday, 11:30 am til 12:30 am; Sunday, noon til 10:00 pm.

MENU SELECTIONS

Appetizers

Bowl of Chili
Mixed Green Salad
Gorgonzola Salad

Entrees

Bearnaise Burger
Caviar & Sour Cream Burger
Gorgonzola Cheese Burger
Hollywood Burger with Avocado & Sprouts
Beef or Chicken Fajitas

Desserts

Chocolate Decadent
Hot Fudge Walnut Sundae
Strawberry Rhubarb Pie

HARVEY'S CHELSEA RESTAURANT
108 West 18th Street
New York, N.Y. 10011
(212) 243-5644

The 42' red mahogany bar with cut crystal and brass saloon clock was built on the premises by Anheuser-Busch.

Open 7 days a week for brunch, lunch and dinner.
Reservations are suggested.
Private rooms available for 10-150.
American Express.

MENU SELECTIONS

Appetizers

Baked Brie
Smoked Trout

Entrees

Shepherd's Pie
Venison Stew
Oysters pan saute in lemon, butter & parsley
Prime Ribs of Beef au jus
Mixed Grill

Desserts

Carrot Walnut Cake
Pecan Pie

IL CORTILE
Ristorante Italiano
125 Mulberry Street
New York, N.Y. 10013
(212) 226-6060

A landmark in Little Italy. Regional Italian cooking, Roman Florentine ambiance.

Monday - Thursday 12 - 12; Friday & Saturday 1 pm - 12 am.
Reservations suggested.
All major credit cards.

MENU SELECTIONS

Appetizers

Gamberi e Calamari soft' Aceto
Insalata ai Fratti di Mare
Croquette e Frittelle

Main Course

Palafitta
Gamberi e Seppie allo Spiedo
La Valdostana Originale
Il Seno di Venere
Pollo allo Champagne

Desserts

Torta al Quattro Forraggi

JOANNA
18 East 18th Street
New York, N.Y. 10003
(212) 675-7900

The finest bistro fare, featuring seasonal specialities and extravagant desserts, served in a handsome turn-of-the-century setting.

Open Monday - Thursday, noon - midnight; Friday & Saturday, noon - 1:00 am; Sunday, noon - 10:00 pm.
Special weekend brunch, noon - 4:00 pm.

Chef de Cuisine Etienne Lizzi
American Express, Mastercard, Visa.

MENU SELECTIONS

Appetizers

Terrine of Country Game
Gravalax with Dill Sauce
Petrossian Caviar

Entrees

Paupiette of Pacific Salmon
Tournedos Rossini
Seafood Pasta Genova
Grilled Dover Sole Hollandaise

Desserts

Chocolate Bourbon Cake
Fruit Tart

THE NIGHTCLUB
Downstairs at Joanna
18 East 18th Street
New York, N.Y. 10003
(212) 675-7100

Sophisticated, intimate nightclub featuring dancing, the finest spirits, champagne and caviar til 4:00 am.

Open Thursday, Friday & Saturday. $10.00 minimum.
Available for all private occasions.
Expert specialized planning for all corporate and personal functions.
American Express, Mastercard, Visa.

THE JOCKEY CLUB

112 Central Park South
New York, N.Y. 10019
(212) 757-1900 Ext. 7500

An 18th Century decor prevails in The Jockey Club Restaurant and Bar, with wood paneling, working fireplaces and a private collection of oil paintings providing a lovely setting for gracious dining. Featuring international cuisine and an extensive wine list, The Jockey Club offers a truly great dining experience.

Breakfast 7 am - 10 am (Monday - Sunday); Continental Breakfast 10 am - 11 am (Monday - Sunday); Luncheon 12 pm - 2:30 pm (Monday - Saturday); Dinner 6 pm - 11 pm (Monday - Saturday, on Sundays until 10 pm); Brunch 12 pm - 2:30 pm (Saturday and Sunday); Jockey Club Bar and Cocktail Lounge 12 pm - 1 pm (Daily).
Reservations are requested.
All major credit cards.

MENU SELECTIONS

Appetizers

Assorted Hors D'Oeuvres
Terrines & Pates
Ravioli Filled with Lobster
Lobster Bisque

Entrees

Dover Sole Poche Ambassador
Quenelles of Pike Lyonnaise
Noisettes of Veal, Tarragon Sauce
Poularde au Champagne

Desserts

Chocolate, Grand Marnier,
Strawberry & Jockey Club
Hot Souffles

KEENS
72 West 36th Street
New York, N.Y. 10018
(212) 947-3636

A stunning restoration of an authentic turn-of-the-century New York City restaurant. Keens is famed for its legendary mutton chops, the world's largest clay pipe collection, as well as its exquisite interior spaces. The private party rooms are popular with corporate customers. Elegant American cuisine.

Open Monday - Friday, 11:45 am - 11:00 pm; Saturday 5:00 pm to 11 pm; Closed Sunday.
Reservations are suggested.
All major credit cards.

MENU SELECTIONS

Appetizers

Little Neck Clams on the Half Shell
Arugola, Romaine & Goat Cheese Salad
Homemade Ravioli with Duck & Wild Mushrooms

Entrees

Mutton Chop, mint butter
Beef Wellington
Sauteed Calf Liver with Green Peppercorns
Sauteed Breast of Chicken with Pommery Mustard
Sauteed Shrimp with Wild Mushrooms

Desserts

Deep Dish Apple Pie
Homemade Ice Cream

LANDMARK TAVERN LTD.
Established 1868
626 11th Avenue
New York, N.Y. 10036
(212) 757-8595

Originally a waterfront saloon, today's Landmark Tavern echoes its mid-19th century atmosphere with pressed tin ceilings, mahogany bar, tiled floor and pot-bellied stoves. An upstairs dining room is available.

Reservations suggested.
Open 7 days a week offering lunch & dinner, Saturday & Sunday brunch.
American Express.

MENU SELECTIONS

Appetizers

Irish Potato Soup with Bacon
Grilled Wild Mushrooms
Mixed Greens with Warm Grilled Chicken Breast

Entrees

Shepherds Pie
Fish & Chips
Bangers and Mash
Grilled Fresh Fish
Lamb Steak
Grilled Scallops and Irish Bacon on a Skewer
Roast Prime Ribs of Beef au jus
with Yorkshire Pudding

Desserts

Brownie Pie
Chocolate Mousse Pie
Bourbon Walnut Pie

LAURENT
Maison Fondée 1951
111 East 56th Street
New York, N.Y. 10022
(212) 753-2729

Laurent's menu changes daily and features prime seasonal specialties: "When it's first in season, it's first at Laurent!" Bar and cocktail lounge, award-winning wine cellar, garden dining room, private parties from 10 to 100.

Open for lunch Monday - Friday, 12 - 3 pm; Dinner Monday - Friday, 6 - 10:30 pm; Saturday 5 - 11 pm; Sunday 5 - 10:30 pm. Reservations are required.
All major credit cards.

MENU SELECTIONS

Appetizers

Crepes Laurent
Foie Gras Truffé
Soupe à l'Oignon au Gratin

Entrees

Red Snapper Grille au Citron Vert Celeri Braise
Poulet Saute à l'Espagnole
Feuilletè de Homard Laurent
Steak au Poivre Flambe à l'Armagnac
Long Island Duckling à l'Orange

Desserts

Mousse au Chocolat
Souffles Tous Parfums

LAVIN'S
23 West 39th Street
New York, N.Y. 10018
(212) 921-1288

Lavin's celebrates American cuisine with artful presentations of the freshest fish, meats, poultry and garden ingredients. Each day, a selection of wines and champagnes is available by the taste and glass from Lavin's extensive wine list. Lavin's chestnut panelled turn-of-the-century dining room was formerly a private men's club built by Andrew Carnegie.

Open Monday through Friday, noon until midnight
Reservations are required.
All major credit cards. Available for private parties.

MENU SELECTIONS

Appetizers

Mesquite Carpaccio
Salmon Tartare

Entrees

Pan Roasted Saddle of Rabbit
Roast Quail Stuffed with Cous-cous and Currants
Mesquite grilled loin of lamb
Sauteed Breast of Duck, sliced

Desserts

Fresh Selection Daily

LION'S ROCK
316 East 77th Street
New York, N.Y. 10021
(212) 988-3610

Situated on a favorite picnic spot once known as Jones Wood, legendary location of buried treasure and a Kissing Bridge, the focal point of the garden is a massive outcropping of red granite from the glacier age.

Lunch Monday - Friday 11:30 am - 3 pm
Dinner every night 5 pm - midnight
Saturday & Sunday Brunch
Private Party Accommodations Available
Reservations suggested.
All major credit cards.

MENU SELECTIONS

Appetizers

Sesame Grilled Salmon, Mustard Greens
Chicken, Black Forest Ham & Tarragon Sausage
Fresh Tuna Paillard, Orange & Ginger Butter

Entrees

Poached Eastern Shore Halibut
Medallions of Lamb
Lobster & Sea Scallops Fricassee
Tenderloin of Roast Pork
Saddle of Venison

Desserts

Black Velvet Chocolate Torte
Fresh Apple Tart
Homemade Sorbet

LA LOUISIANA
132 Lexington Avenue
New York, N.Y. 10016
(212) 686-3959

La Louisiana, one of the first restaurants to celebrate American cuisine in New York, specializes in the Cajun food of southwest Louisiana. Crawfish, catfish and shrimp are flown in fresh from the Gulf Coast, prepared in both traditional and innovative ways, and served in a charming and intimate dining room.

Open Monday - Thursday, 6 - 11 pm; Friday & Saturday, 6 - 12 pm.
Reservations are suggested.
American Express and Diners Club.

MENU SELECTIONS

Appetizers

Boudin
Crudité de Boeuf
Gumbo du Jour

Entrees

Filet of Pork de la Houssaye
Stolen Blackened Fish
Catfish
Southern Fried Steak
Fresh Louisiana Crawfish (in season)

Desserts

Varied Selections

MAXWELL'S PLUM
64th Street and First Avenue
New York, N.Y. 10021
(212) 628-2100

Maxwell's Plum opened in 1966 and has since become one of the most famous restaurants in the world. Famed tiffany glass ceiling and unique decor make it one of New York's most stunning restaurants. The cuisine has won rave reviews and the wine list is one of the finest in the country. Popular with both New Yorkers and visitors.

Open for Lunch Monday through Friday noon - 5:00 pm; Brunch Saturday noon - 5:00 pm, Sunday 11 am - 5:00 pm; Dinner Sunday through Thursday 5:00 pm - 12:30 am, Friday and Saturday 5:00 pm - 1:30 am; Pre-theatre Monday through Saturday 5:00 - 7:00 pm ($13.50). Available for private parties.
Reservations recommended.
All major credit cards.

MENU SELECTIONS

Appetizers

Sauteed New York Duck Liver
Steamed Mussels Mariniere
Mesquite Grilled Tuna Carpaccio

Entrees

Black Pepper Fettucine
Grilled Swordfish
Whole Roasted Florida Red Snapper
Spareribs Glazed with Honey & Ginger
Medallions of Venison

Desserts

Pecan Tartlet
Chocolate Raspberry Terrine
Blueberry Buckle

MANHATTAN CAFE
1161 First Avenue (at 64th Street)
New York, N.Y. 10021
(212) 888-6556

THE STEAKHOUSE WITH A DIFFERENCE. Thick sirloins, chops, jumbo lobsters, seafood and Continental specialties.

Serving lunch, Monday - Friday from noon. Brunch Saturday and Sunday from 11:30 am. Dinner seven days.
Reservations are suggested.
All major credit cards.

MENU SELECTIONS

Appetizers

Jumbo Shrimp Cocktail
Baked Clams Oreganata
Smoked Atlantic Salmon

Entrees

Prime New York Sirloin Steak
Porterhouse Steak
Veal Chop
Jumbo Lobster

Desserts

Manhattan Cake
Napoleon
Rum Cake

MORAN'S CHELSEA SEAFOOD RESTAURANT
146 Tenth Avenue, at 19th Street
New York, N.Y. 10011
(212) 989-9225

Moran's, famed for its fabulous seafood specialties, is a charming restoration of a turn of the century waterfront saloon. The five dining rooms, wood burning fireplaces and patio garden blend beautifully to create a unique historical Chelsea restaurant, located on the former site of the Clement Moore Estate. Parties and catering.

Open seven days, noon to midnight.
Reservations are recommended.
All major credit cards.

MENU SELECTIONS

Appetizers

Smoked Brook Trout
Steamed Clams

Entrees

Live Maine Lobsters up to 4½ lbs.
Rack of Lamb
Salmon Wellington
Bouillabaise
Red Snapper in Pappilote

Desserts

Fresh Selection Daily

THE ODEON
145 West Broadway
New York, N.Y. 10013
(212) 233-0507

Lunch: Noon to 3 pm, Monday - Friday; Daily Dinner: 7 pm - 12:30 am; Supper: 1 am - 2:30 am; Sunday Brunch, Noon - 3:30.
Reservations recommended.
American Express, Visa, Mastercard.

MENU SELECTIONS

Appetizers

Warm Chevre Salad
Four Poached Wellfleet Oysters
Homemade Fettuccine with Fresh Shrimp

Entrees

Grilled Sea Scallops
Cassoulet
Pan Sauteed Filet Mignon
Roasted Loin Lamb Chops

Desserts

Chocolate Framboise Cake
Very Special Apple Tart
Lemon Tart

OH HO SO
395 West Broadway
New York, N.Y. 10012
(212) 966-6110

Cantonese cuisine in casual elegance.

Open Monday - Friday, noon til midnight; Saturday & Sunday, noon til 1:00 am.
Reservations recommended.
American Express, Diners Club.

MENU SELECTIONS

Appetizers

Fried Coconut Prawns
Honey Glazed Barbecue Pork
Oh Ho So Egg Roll

Entrees

Spicy Snow Pea Chicken
Roast Plum Duckling
Sauteed Filet of Sole with Garlic & Black Bean Sauce
Lobster Special fried with Ginger
Lobster Fried Rice

Desserts

Fresh Selection Daily

ONE FIFTH
One Fifth Avenue
New York, N.Y. 10003
(212) 260-3434

We have rescued the first class dining room of the RMS Caronia, the fabled Cunard liner which sank in 1974 during a typhoon in the South China Sea. The ship is gone; you, however, may dine in its former splendor.

Open for lunch, noon til 3:00 pm; Saturday brunch, noon til 4:00 pm; Sunday brunch, 11:00 am - 4:30 pm. Dinner Monday - Friday, 6:00 - 11:30 pm, Saturday & Sunday, 6:30 pm til 12:30 am.
Bar open til 4:00 am.
Reservations are suggested.
All major credit cards.

MENU SELECTIONS

Appetizers

Tropical Fruit with Prosciutto
and Smoked Mozzarella
Chilled Sea Scallops with Grapefruit
Lobster Consumme

Entrees

Grilled Black Angus Steak, Green Peppercorn Sauce
Saffron Fish Stew
Sauteed Medallions of Tuna, Orange Sage Sauce
Swordfish Steak, Truffle and Herb Butter
Fresh Linguine with Lobser and Mushrooms

Desserts

Bananas Foster Flambe
Chocolate Mousse with Tuille
Honey Poached Pear
with Strawberry Raspberry Sauce

ONE IF BY LAND, TWO IF BY SEA
17 Barrow Street
Greenwich Village, N.Y. 10014
(212) 228-0822

Continental cuisine served in a beautifuly restored 18th century landmark carriage house formerly owned by Aaron Burr.

Open 7 days a week 4:00 pm - 4:00 am serving cocktails with piano music from 4:00 pm. Dinner from 5:30 pm til 12:00 am Sunday - Thursday & from 5:30 pm til 1:00 am Friday & Saturday.
Reservations recommended.
All major credit cards.

MENU SELECTIONS

Appetizers

Crepes, Fruit de Mer, Gratinée
Escargots, Rapa Nui
Smoked Nova Scotia Salmon, garni

Entrees

Charcoal Broiled Veal Chop, Zingara
Emincé of Chicken Breast, Florentine
Crisp Long Island Duckling, au Porto
Chateaubriand, Garni, for Two
Shrimp, Sauté a la Maison

Desserts

Fresh Selection Daily

THE OYSTER BAR & RESTAURANT
Grand Central Station
Lower Level
New York, N.Y. 10017
(212) 490-6650

"The fish is fresh, carefully prepared, and served piping hot."
—★★★*New York Times*

"Recently opened and refurbished, this cavernous landmark is better than ever."
—★★★*New York Magazine*

"Famous far and wide for the best seafood in the city. The food is extraordinary."
—VVVV *The Village Voice*

Open Monday - Friday, 11:30 am - 9:30 pm.
Reservations are suggested.
All major credit cards.

MENU SELECTIONS

Appetizers

Smoked Salmon
Daily Selection of 6-12 different oysters on the half shell
Blanquette de Belons aux Poireaux

Entrees

Florida Red Snapper Salad
Medallion of Canadian Lotte with chunks of Fresh Maine Lobster
Broiled Extra large Gulf of Maine Sea Scallops
Bouillabaisse
Bluefish Filet
Mako Shark

Desserts

Strawberry Rhubarb Tart
Dutch Almond Crescent
Whole Wheat Apple Pie

PEACOCK ALLEY
The Waldorf-Astoria
301 Park Avenue at 50th Street
New York, N.Y. 10022
(212) 872-4895

Peacock Alley, noted for celebrity watching, is off the main lobby of New York's famed Waldorf-Astoria. The restaurant serves American and continental cuisine. It is home of Cole Porter's own piano, played nightly for cocktails and dining.

Open for breakfast, lunch, dinner and cocktails, 7 am - 2 pm.
Sunday brunch, 11 am - 2:45 pm.
Reservations are recommended.
All major credit cards.

MENU SELECTIONS

Appetizers

Ensemble of Seafood Cocktail
Warm Salad of Quail and Fresh Foie Gras
Porcini Tortellini with Sun Dried Tomato

Entees

Grilled English Sole with Crayfish Tails
Lobster and Scallop Crepes, Watercress Sauce, Glazed Bearnaise
Medallions of Veal, Sauce of Selected Wild Mushrooms
Broiled Prime Sirloin Steak Bernaise

Desserts

Seasonal Berries, Melons
Caramel Custard

LES PLEIADES Restaurant
20 East 76th Street
New York, N.Y. 10021
(212) 535-7230

Called the "art world club," and located amidst the Madison Avenue galleries and museums, this fine French restaurant has for 15 years been a favorite gathering place for artists, museum people, art dealers and auction house members.

Open Monday - Saturday, serving lunch 12 - 3 pm, dinner 5:30 - 11 pm.
Reservations are recommended.
All major credit cards.

MENU SELECTIONS

Appetizers

L'Artichaut en Feuilles
Les Pates Assortis Pleiades
Les Escargots Forestieres

Entrees

La Sole Anglaise Grille Sauce Moutarde
Le Steak Au Poivre Des Iles Malgaches
La Noix De Ris De Veau Aux Morilles
La Truite Fraiche Meuniere
La Poulet Roti a L'Estragon

Desserts

Les Desserts Du Jour ou Fromage
Le Souffle Au Grand Marnier

THE QUILTED GIRAFFE
955 Second Avenue
New York, N.Y. 10022
(212) 753-5355

Luxurious, elegant, expensive, sophisticated. Innovative, always changing menu with a French influence. The chef-owner and his wife are always present to assure your complete satisfaction.

Open Monday - Friday, 5:45 - 10:15 pm.
Reservations are essential.
American Express, Diners Club

MENU SELECTIONS

Pre Fix Dinner

Wild Mushroom and Truffle Soup
Lobster with Potatoes in Creamy Herb Sauce

Seared Japanese Tuna
with Potato Sauce and Red Pepper Puree
Confit of Duck with Bacon Potatoes
Steak with White Beans and Sausage

Selections from our Cheese Cart

Pecan Square Served Warm with Whipped Cream
Creme Brulee

RAOUL'S
182 Prince Street
New York, N.Y. 10012
(212) 966-3518

Authentic French bistro in Soho, serving classical fare.

Open 7 days, 6:30 - 11:30 pm.
Reservations suggested.
American Express, Mastercard, Visa.

MENU SELECTIONS

Appetizers

Ris de veau en Salade
Marinade de Poissons
Huitres mignonette

Entrees

St. Pierre au foie de canard
Thon à la bordelaise
Caille farcie sauce morille
Steak au poivre
Carré d'agneau aux Herbes

Desserts

Torte à la framboise
Gratin de fruits

LE REGINETTE
69 East 59th Street
New York, N.Y. 10022
(212) 758-0530

Le Reginette, Regine's bistro, corner of 59th Street and Park Avenue, features French cuisine with Moroccan specialities.

Cocktails 5 - 8 pm, with complimentary buffet, cruvinet wine bar; Marrakesh Express Brunch every Saturday.
Available for private parties.

Open for lunch and dinner, Monday - Saturday, noon - midnight.
Reservations recommended.
All major credit cards.

MENU SELECTIONS

Appetizers

Le Trio de Fettuccini á la Creme
de Tomotes et Poivrons Doux
La Terrine de Venaison á l'Eau de Vie
de Cerise, Sauce Cumberland
La Salade de Radiccio et Mozzarella

Entrees

L'Escalope de Saumon aux Deux Caviars
Les Filet de Sole et Médaillons de Homard
la Valliére
Les Médaillons de Veau au Beurre Acidulé

Desserts

Le Pavé au Chocolat au Coulis de Menthe
La Tulipe de Fraises Chaudes au Poivre
sur Glace de Vanille

THE RIVER CLUB
Burd Street & Hudson River
Nyack, New York 10960
(914) 358-0220

The River Club, a picturesque restaurant on the shores of the Hudson River in the quaint antique-filled village of Nyack, only 24 miles from midtown Manhattan. Specializing in regional American cuisine with a dockside veranda for outdoor dining and cocktails.

Open Tuesday - Sunday, lunch noon til 3:00 pm; dinner 6:00 - 10:00 pm.
Reservations are not accepted.
All major credit cards.

MENU SELECTIONS

Appetizers

Clam Chowder
Vegetables Tempura
Tortellini Carbonara

Entrees

Chicken & Shrimp Brochette
Sirloin Steak
Paneed Veal and Pasta
Baked Scrod
Beer Batter Shrimp

Desserts

Fresh Selection Daily

ROEBLING'S
11 Fulton Street, South Street Seaport
New York, N.Y. 10038
(212) 608-3980

Roebling's, with its expansive mahogany and brass bars, is a favorite with the Wall Street crowd, as well as visitors to the historic South Street Seaport. The cuisine is Regional American, with many fresh seafood specialties. Free buffet Monday - Friday at cocktail hour. (Fridays are legendary!)

Open daily, 11:30 am til 2:00 am. Sunday Brunch til 5:00 pm.
Reservations are recommended.
Available for private parties.
All major credit cards.

MENU SELECTIONS

Appetizers

Crab Puffs with Cajun Remoulade
Escargot sauteed with Spinach, Tomato, Potato and Herbs
Bluepoint Oysters on the half shell

Entrees

Bluefish Broiled with Ginger, Scallions and Soy Sauce
Cajun Chicken
Grilled Marinated Swordfish with Herb Butter
Linguine with Shrimp, Scallops, Clams and Mussels Marinara
Grilled Filet Mignon with Sauce Bernaise

Desserts

Fresh Selection Daily

ROXANNE'S
158 Eighth Avenue (at 18th Street)
New York, N.Y. 10011
(212) 741-2455

Fine innovative French/American cuisine. Intimate, multi-level dining with lush, open air garden.

Serving Lunch Monday through Friday, 12 - 2:30 pm;
Dinner Monday through Saturday, 6 - 11:30 pm.
Reservations recommended.
Visa, Mastercard.

MENU SELECTIONS

Appetizers

Sauteed Wild Mushroom in Puff Pastry
Ricotta & Crabmeat Ravioli
in Tomato Court Bouillon
Fresh Norwegian Salmon Gravlax

Entrees

Tournedos of Beef with Zinfandel Wine Sauce
Poached Medallions of Lotte
in White Wine Creme Fraiche
Sauteed Calf's Liver
with Sweet/Sour Margaux Sauce
Long Island Bouillabaisse

Desserts

Turnover of sweet cheese, nut & raisin
in phyllo pastry with raspberry coulis
Chocolate Cake Rennie with Whipped Cream

RUSSELL'S
At the Sheraton-Russell Hotel
100 East 37th Street
New York, N.Y. 10016
(212) 685-1727

Located in historic Murray Hill, dine where Mary Murray detained General Howe in 1776. Featuring traditional American cuisine, with seafood specialties.

Open for breakfast, Monday - Friday, 7 - 11 am; Saturday & Sunday, 7:30 - 11:30 am; lunch, Monday - Friday, 12 noon - 2:30 pm, Saturday & Sunday brunch, 12 noon - 3 pm; dinner 7 days, 6 - 10 pm. Reservations are suggested.
All major credit cards.

MENU SELECTIONS

Appetizers

Angel Hair Pasta with Lobster Medallions
Baked Oysters
Gravlax over Leaf Spinach

Entrees

Swordfish Cutlet
Salmon Filet
Sea Trout
Twin Filet of Beef Normandie
Baby Rack of Lamb

Desserts

Fresh Selection Daily

65 IRVING PLACE
Corner of 18th Street
New York, N.Y. 10003
(212) 673-3939

Located on a quiet, little-known street just south of Gramercy Park is this romantic restaurant. The lace curtains, hanging plants, cheerful wallpaper and profusion of fresh flowers create an enchanting atmosphere. The changing menu is an inventive blend of French and Italian cuisines, featuring seasonal specialties. An added bonus to dining here is the sidewalk cafe, open during warm weather.

Open for lunch Monday - Saturday, 12 noon - 3 pm; Sunday brunch, 12 noon - 4 pm; dinner Monday - Thursday, 6 - 11:30 pm, Friday & Saturday til midnight.
Reservations are suggested.
All major credit cards.

MENU SELECTIONS

Appetizers

Roulade of Sun-dried Tomatoes, Mozzarella & Pesto
Shitaki Mushrooms & Snails Provencales

Entrees

Veal Scaloppine with Porcini Mushrooms
New Jersey Suckling Pig
& Homemade Apple Sauce
Fish of the Day
Broiled Lamb Chop with Fresh Rosemary
Filet of Beef Wellington

Desserts

Made fresh daily on the premises

SUERKEN'S RESTAURANT
Established 1877
27 Park Place
New York, N.Y. 10007
(212) 267-6389

A landmark restaurant in lower Manhattan. Clam & oyster bar, fresh fish daily, German specialties.

Open Monday - Thursday, 11 am - 10 pm; Friday until 11 pm; Saturday 12 - 7 pm.

MENU SELECTIONS

Appetizers

Cherrystone Clams on the Half Shell
Poached Scallops in Tarragon Cream Sauce
Oysters on the Half Shell
Steamed Littlenecks Espanol
Sauteed Shrimp in a Mustard Chive Sauce

Entrees

Broiled Norwegian or Alaskan Salmon
Grilled Swordfish Steak
Oyster Stew
Sauerbraten, Red Cabbage & Potato Pancakes
Schnitzel a la Holstein, Anchovey & Caper Garni

Desserts

Homemade Apple Strudel with Schlag
Chocolate Pecan Pie
Blueberry Cheesecake

TENNESSEE MOUNTAIN
143 Spring Street
New York, N.Y. 10012
(212) 431-3993

"The Best Ribs in Town"...served in a landmark 1807 farmhouse. Marion Burros, *New York Times* awarded ★★ February, 1984: "It offers the meatiest ribs in town and the freshest, fattest fried onion rings." BBQ chicken, excellent chili and frozen margaritas are among many of the other specialties.

Open Monday - Wednesday, 1:30 am - 11 pm; Thursday - Saturday, 11:30 am - midnight; Sunday 11:30 am - 10 pm.
Reservations recommended.
Private parties available.
All major credit cards.

MENU SELECTIONS

Appetizers

Tennessee Nachos
Coconut Battered Shrimp

Entrees

Barbequed Baby Back Ribs
Barbequed Beef Ribs
Barbequed Chicken
Catch of the Day
Tex Mex Burger

Desserts

Cappucino Pie
Chocolate Blackout Cake
Warm Pecan Pie

TERRACE RESTAURANT

400 West 119th Street
New York, N.Y. 10027
(212) 666-9490

With panoramic views of Manhattan, the Palisades and the George Washington Bridge, and classical music nightly, the Terrace serves classical and nouvelle French cuisine. Free valet parking in the evening.

Open for lunch Tuesday - Friday, 12 noon - 2:30 pm; dinner Tuesday - Thursday, 6 - 10 pm, Friday & Saturday, 6 - 10:30 pm; closed Sunday & Monday for private parties.
Reservations are suggested.
All major credit cards.

MENU SELECTIONS

Appetizers

Mousse of Smoked Trout
Cavier Malossol Beluga
Oysters Poached in Champagne

Entrees

Filet of Striped Bass Poached
with Vegetables & Saffron
Brace of Quail, Partially boned, with Shallots,
Ginger, Fresh Herbs & Balsamic Vinegar
Medaillons of Veal with Morels
& Sweet Onion Mousse
Veal Sweetbreads with Port & Truffles
Game in Season

Desserts

A Selection from the Dessert Wagon

TEXARKANA

64 West 10th Street
New York, N.Y. 10011
(212) 254-5800

Located on historic 10th Street in Greenwich Village, this townhouse has been a meeting place for diners and drinkers for nearly a century. Texarkana serves some of the most critically acclaimed American food in the New York area. Specialties are foods of the Gulf Coast and the Southwest.

Open nightly 6:00 pm til midnight; Tuesday - Saturday til 3:45 am for late night menu.
Reservations are suggested.
American Express and Diners Club.

MENU SELECTIONS

Appetizers

New Orleans-style Salad
Jicama Salad
Cajun Head Cheese

Entrees

Crawfish Etouffee
Barbecued Suckling Pig with Cornbread & Jalapeno Dressing
Texarkana's Real Hot Shrimp
Stolen Blackened Fish
Southern Fried Chicken

Desserts

Fresh Selection Daily

LE TRAIN BLEU
Bloomingdale's
1000 Third Avenue, 6th floor
New York, N.Y. 10022
(212) 705-2100

A nostalgic re-creation of a luxury French railroad dining car. Serving Brunch, Lunch, Tea, Cocktails and Dinner in fine style. New York, N.Y.; King of Prussia, Pa.; Dallas, Tx.

Brunch, Monday - Friday, 11 am - 12 noon; luncheon, Monday - Friday, 12 noon - 3:30 pm; afternoon tea, Monday - Friday, 3:30 - 4:30 pm; Saturday lunch, 12 noon - 4:30 pm; early dinner, Monday & Thursday, til 7:30 pm.
Reservations are suggested.
Available for Private Parties.
American Express, Bloomingdale's, Diners Club.

MENU SELECTIONS

Appetizers

All Natural Vegetable Potage
Chicken Liver Mousse à l'Armagnac
Escargots Forestière en Crouton

Entrees

Poached Salmon, Pommery Hollandaise
Grilled Chicken Breast, Chanterelles
& Apricot Compote
Salad of Spinach, Radicchio & Romaine
Oven Tart of Scallops with Lime & Marjoram
Crisp Fried Shrimp, Sweet Orange Sauce

Desserts

Hot Chocolate Souffle au Grand Marnier
Compote of Quince and Apple, Honey Cream

TRE SCALINI
230 East 58th Street
New York, N.Y. 10022
(212) 688-6888

New York's elite and world celebrities gather here to savor some of the most exquisitely delicate Northern Italian cooking. Rated 3-Stars.

Open Monday - Friday, noon - 3:00 pm, 5:00 pm til midnight; Saturday, 5:00 pm til midnight; closed Sunday.
Reservations are required.
All major credit cards.

MENU SELECTIONS

Appetizers

Trota Affumicata
Assortimento Misto di Pesce Caldo

Pasta

Risotto con Funghi Porcini
Fettuccine Alfredo
Rigatoni con Carciofi

Entrees

Calamari alla Luciana
Pollo alla Diavola
Fegato alla Veneziana
Paillard di Manzo

Desserts

Zabaglione
Fragole Fresche
Gelati Assortiti

VANESSA
289 Bleecker Street
New York, N.Y. 10014
(212) 243-4225

Vanessa, in the heart of Greenwich Village, offers an exceptional experience in the best American nouvelle cuisine. Seasonal dishes using the freshest ingredients are creatively prepared. Domestic wines and spirits add interest for the connoisseur. The atmosphere is soft and romantic, with delicate shades of purple and fuchsia, accented with fresh floral arrangements and deco brass fixtures.

Open 7 days for dinner, 6 pm - whenever. Sunday brunch, Labor Day - Memorial Day.
Reservations are suggested.
All major credit cards.

MENU SELECTIONS

Appetizers

Terrine of New York State Foie Gras
Green Asparagus Salad
Sashimi of Raw Tuna

Entrees

Sauteed Salmon with Four Onions
Red Snapper Sauteed
with Crushed Macadamia Nuts
Loin Veal Chop Grilled with Fresh Sage, Madeira
Grilled Aged Sirloin of Beef
Grilled Duck Breast with Mixed Peppercorns

Desserts

Varied Selections Daily

VICTOR'S CAFÉ 52
236 West 52nd Street
New York, N.Y. 10019
(212) 586-7714

Enjoy a touch of Havana in the heart of New York's theatre district. Come to Victor's Café 52 for a unique dining experience. Savor any of our 54 delicious entrees in one of our skylight rooms and listen to soothing violin and piano music while dining under the stars. Special accommodations for groups.

Open seven days for lunch and dinner.
Reservations are suggested.
All major credit cards.

MENU SELECTIONS

Appetizers

Jumbo Shrimp Cocktail
Mussels in Green Sauce
Black Bean Soup

Entrees

Shredded Beef a la Cubana
Special Paella Valenciana for two
"Duran Victory" Cuban Style Steak
Suckling Roast Pig
Red Snapper Vasca

Desserts

Double Egg Custard
Rice Pudding
Caramel Custard

WINDOWS ON THE WORLD
One World Trade Center
New York, N.Y. 10048
(212) 938-1111

You won't find a restaurant experience like Windows on the World anywhere else in New York. 107 stories high in the clouds, Windows on the World is the perfect place to fall in love with New York. The wine list is exceptional. The cuisine has earned Gault/Millau Guide awards. Free parking within the building.

The Restaurant: open for dinner, Monday - Saturday, 5 - 10 pm; Saturday buffet, 12 noon - 3 pm; Sunday buffet, 12 noon - 7:30 pm. *The Cellar in The Sky:* open Monday - Saturday, 7:30 pm. *The Hors d'Oeuverie:* Open for breakfast, Monday - Friday 7:30 am - 10:30 am. Open Monday - Saturday, 3 pm - 1 am; Sunday brunch, 12 noon - 3 pm.

Reservations are required for *The Restaurant, Cellar in the Sky*, and Sunday brunch *(Hors d'Oeuverie).*
All major credit cards.

MENU SELECTIONS

Appetizers

Pesto Agnolotti in Cream
with Shiitake Mushrooms and Herbs
Gratin of Sea Scallops in Riesling
with Leeks and Sorrel

Entrees

Grilled Scallop of Salmon with Basil Beurre Blanc
and Corn Meal Pasta
Shrimp Sautéed with Mustard, Coriander
and Tiny Vegetables
Roast Veal Tenderloin with Tarragon Sauce
and Onion Purée
Rack of Young Lamb, James Beard
Swordfish Steak, Orange Tarragon butter

Desserts

Figs Poached in Port
with Homemade Walnut Ice Cream
Hazelnut Dacquoise

Notes

Notes

Restaurants by Cuisine

American
Binghamton's
Gage & Tollner
Hamburger Harry's
Harvey's Chelsea Restaurant
Keens
The Landmark Tavern
La Louisiana
The River Club
Roebling's
Russell's
Tennessee Mountain
Texarkana

Cafe
Caffe Roma

Chinese
Dish of Salt
Oh Ho So

Continental/New American
Berry's
Cafe Luxembourg
Garvin's
Joanna
The Jockey Club
Lavin's
Lion's Rock
Maxwell's Plum
The Odeon
One Fifth
One If By Land, Two If By Sea
Peacock Alley
The Quilted Giraffe
Roxanne's
65 Irving Place
Vanessa
Windows on the World

Cuban
Victor's Café 52

French
The Black Sheep
The Carlyle Restaurant
La Colombe d'Or
Le Cygne
Laurent
Les Pleiades
Raoul's
Le Reginette
The Terrace Restaurant
Le Train Bleu

German
Suerken's

Greek
Avgerino's

Italian
Angelo's
Barbetta
Gian Marino
Il Cortile
Tre Scalini

Mediterranean
Andrée's Mediterranean Cuisine

Mexican
Caramba
Cinco de Mayo
Fonda La Paloma

Seafood/Steaks
Claire
Fay & Allen's Catch of the Sea
Gage & Tollner
Keens
Manhattan Cafe
Moran's
The Oyster Bar & Restaurant
Roebling's
Suerken's

Restaurants by Location

Downtown
Hamburger Harry's
The Odeon
Roebling's
Suerken's
Windows on the World

Little Italy
Angelo's
Caffe Roma
Il Cortile

Soho
Berry's
Cinco de Mayo
Oh Ho So
Raoul's
Tennessee Mountain

Greenwich Village
The Black Sheep
Caramba II
Garvin's
One Fifth
One If By Land, Two If By Sea
Texarkana
Vanessa

Chelsea/Westside 14th - 34th St.
Claire
Harvey's Chelsea Restaurant
Moran's
Roxanne's

Westside 34th - 59th Sts.
Barbetta
Caramba I
Dish of Salt
Hamburger Harry's
The Jockey Club
Keens
The Landmark Tavern
Lavin's
Victor's Café 52

Upper Westside Above 59th St.
Cafe Luxembourg
Caramba III
The Terrace Restaurant

Eastside 14th - 34th Sts.
La Colombe d'Or
Joanna
Joanna (The Nightclub)
La Louisiana
65 Irving Place

Eastside 34th - 59th Sts.
Avgerino's
Le Cygne
Fonda La Paloma
Gian Marino
Laurent
The Oyster Bar & Restaurant
Peacock Alley
The Quilted Giraffe
Le Reginette
Russell's
Le Train Bleu
Tre Scalini

Eastside Above 59th St.
Andrée's Mediterranean Cuisine
The Carlyle Restaurant
Fay & Allen's Catch of the Sea
Lion's Rock
Manhattan Cafe
Maxwell's Plum
Les Pleiades

Brooklyn
Gage & Tollner

Out of Town
Binghamton's
The River Club

Restaurants by Price

Listed below is the price range for dinner entrees at each restaurant, as well as those offering a prix fixe menu. Please note that prices vary seasonally, and the actual cost of any meal depends upon the quantity and quality of appetizers, salads, desserts, beverage, tax and gratuity.

Andrée's Mediterranean Cuisine $19-25
Angelo's $9-15
Avgerino's $9-14
Barbetta $18-29
Berry's $12-18
Binghamton's $9-18
Black Sheep .... $21-30 prix fixe
Cafe Luxembourg $13-21
Caffe Roma $2-5
Caramba $7-12
The Carlyle Restaurant $17-25
Cinco de Mayo $9-14
Claire $9-15
La Colombe d'Or $14-24
Le Cygne .... $49.75 prix fixe
Dish of Salt $14-21
Fay & Allen's Catch of the Sea $19-25
Fonda La Paloma $11-15
Gage & Tollner $9-17
Garvin's $12-18
Gian Marino $12-22
Hamburger Harry's $3-8
Harvey's Chelsea Restaurant $9-17
Il Cortile $11-17
Joanna $12-24
Joanna (The Nightclub) .... $10 minimum
The Jockey Club $22-27
Keens $14-24
The Landmark Tavern $9-18
Laurent $20-30
Lavin's $18-23
Lion's Rock $14-20
La Louisiana $14-25
Maxwell's Plum $12-22
Manhattan Cafe $14-28
Moran's $12-17
The Odeon $14-26
Oh Ho So $12-16
One Fifth $14-19
One If By Land, Two If By Sea $13-27
The Oyster Bar & Restaurant $18-23
Peacock Alley .... $26-35, $33 prix fixe
Les Pleiades $14-24
The Quilted Giraffe .... $75 prix fixe
Raoul's $14-19
Le Reginette $16-19
The River Club $9-16
Roebling's $9-18
Roxanne's $14-23
Russell's $15-19
65 Irving Place $10-18
Suerken's $9-16
Tennessee Mountain $6-12
The Terrace Restaurant $19-26
Texarkana $14-22
Le Train Bleu $11-15
Tre Scalini $13-22
Vanessa $19-24
Victor's Café 52 .... $11-19
Windows on the World $19-24